Where Am I?

LEARNING RIDDLES

Where Am I?
LEARNING RIDDLES

by Peter Ziebel

SCHOLASTIC INC. Cartwheel B·O·O·K·S ®
New York Toronto London Auckland Sydney
Mexico City New Delhi Hong Kong

To my family.
—P.Z.

Copyright © 1999 by Peter Ziebel.
All rights reserved. Published by Scholastic Inc.
SCHOLASTIC, CARTWHEEL BOOKS and associated logos
are trademarks and/or registered trademarks of Scholastic Inc.

Library of Congress Cataloging-in-Publication Data

Ziebel, Peter.
     Where am I?: learning riddles / by Peter Ziebel.
       p.   cm.
     Summary: A collection of simple, rhyming riddles that challege the reader's perspective.
     ISBN 0-590-63599-9
     1. Riddles, Juvenile.   [1. Riddles]   I. Title
     PN6371.5.Z45   1999
     818'.5402--dc21

                                       98-48462
                                          CIP
                                          AC

12 11 10 9 8 7 6 5 4 3 2 1   02 03 04

Printed in the U.S.A.
First printing, September 1999

For a sweet treat,
don't go far.
Just look inside
the . . .

cookie jar.

Am I behind bars?
You may ask.
I'm playing ball
in a . . .

catcher's mask.

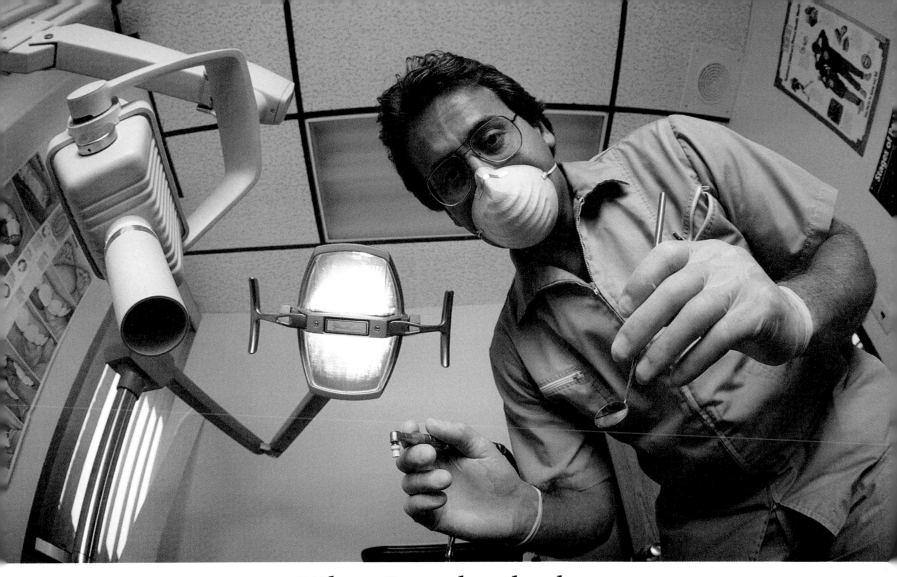

When I need a check-up,
you'll find me there.
Up, up it goes.
It's the . . .

dentist's chair.

I am wet.
I am cool.
I'll come up for air.
I'm in a . . .

swimming pool.

Inside or out?
Just turn the page.
See the birdie . . .

in its cage.

Name this place,
if you are able.
I see legs.
I'm under a . . .

table.

Is that a giant?
Or am I small as a mouse?
Who stands outside this . . .

dollhouse.

You can sit in a garden
for many hours.
But I'm in my house!
I'm holding . . .

flowers.

Here's a long hose—
now we're in luck!
Can you hear its siren?
It's a . . .

fire truck.

I fly through the air
without even one wing.
What helps me to glide?
I'm on a . . .

playground swing.